WRITER'S
TOOLBOX

WORDS, WIT, AND WONDER

Writing Your Own Poem

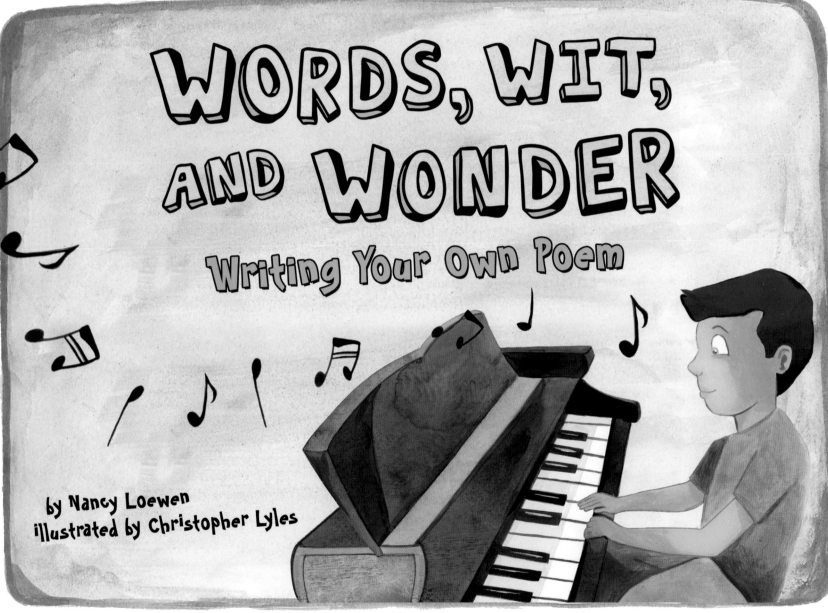

by Nancy Loewen
illustrated by Christopher Lyles

PICTURE WINDOW BOOKS
Minneapolis, Minnesota

Editor: Jill Kalz
Designers: Abbey Fitzgerald and Nathan Gassman
Page Production: Melissa Kes
Editorial Director: Nick Healy
The illustrations in this book were created
with mixed media on illustration board.

Picture Window Books
A Capstone Imprint
151 Good Counsel Drive
P.O. Box 669
Mankato, MN 56002-0669
877-845-8392
www.capstonepub.com

Printed in the United States of America in North Mankato,
Minnesota. 082010 005919R

Library of Congress Cataloging-in-Publication Data
Loewen, Nancy, 1964-
Words, wit, and wonder : writing your own poem /
by Nancy Loewen ; illustrated by Christopher Lyles.
p. cm. — (Writer's Toolbox)
Includes index.
ISBN 978-1-4048-5344-7 (library binding)
ISBN 978-1-4048-5345-4 (paperback)
1. Poetry—Authorship. I. Lyles, Christopher, 1977- II. Title.
PN1059.A9L64 2009
808.1—dc22   2008040590

Special thanks to our adviser, Terry Flaherty, Ph.D.,
Professor of English, Minnesota State University, Mankato,
for his expertise.

Poetry is all around. It's in the nursery rhymes we learn when we're very young. It's in the songs we sing and the books we read.

Poetry ...

Plays with words and plants ideas ...
Opens our eyes and our
Ears ...
Twirls words into
Riddles, ribbons, and raindrops, and makes us say ...
Yes!

—Nancy Loewen

How are poems different from other kinds of writing?

For one thing, poems are usually written in short lines. They often rhyme, or have a set rhythm. Poems connect with our feelings and imaginations.

Poems can be funny or serious. They can tell a story or a joke. Or they might simply show us things from everyday life.

Let's take a look at some of the tools that poets use to create their work.

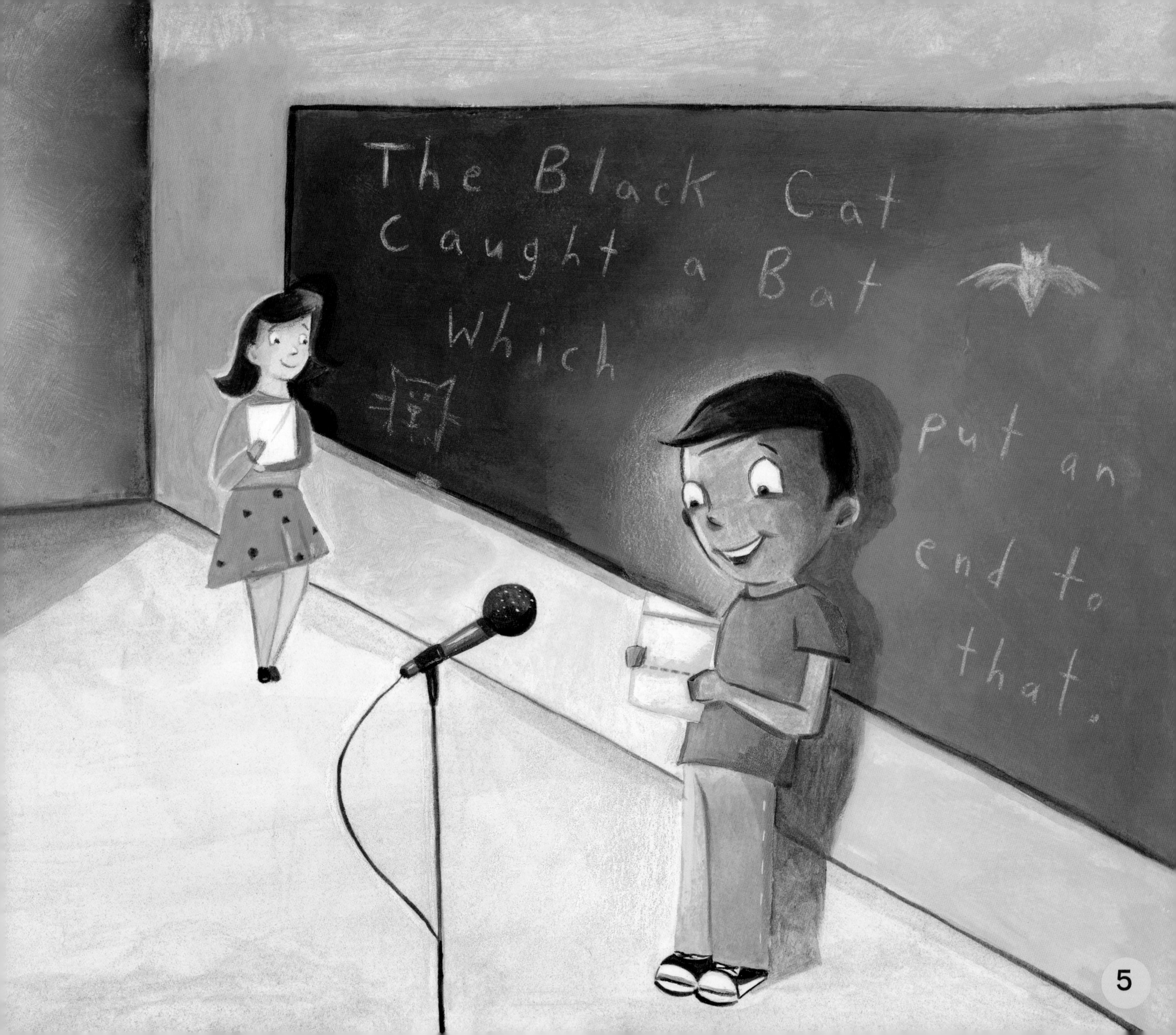
The Black Cat
Caught a Bat
Which
put an
end to
that.

~ Tool 1 ~

RHYTHM is important in music, and it's important in poetry, too. Think of every syllable as a beat—a tap on a drum. Some drumbeats are hard and loud. Some are soft. Together, the hard and soft beats form a pattern.

To hear rhythm in action, read the poem on the opposite page out loud. In the first line, say the words *was*, *Man*, and *beard* louder than the others. In the second line, say the words *said*, *just*, and *feared* louder. The pattern you hear is the poem's rhythm!

There was an Old Man with a beard,
Who said, "It is just as I feared!
Two Owls and a Hen,
Four Larks and a Wren,
Have all built their nests in my beard!"

—Edward Lear

~ Tool 2 ~

RHYME is often used to create rhythm. Rhyming words end with the same sound, like *cat* and *rat*, or *please* and *breeze*. In rhyming poems, the rhyming words come at the ends of lines.

In "Firefly," the words *by* and *sky* rhyme. So do *it* and *lit*. See how *wings* is repeated at the end of the third and sixth lines? It's not a rhyme, since it's the same word. But repeating the word works the same as a rhyme, and it brings the poem to a good close.

Firefly

A little light is going by,
Is going up to see the sky,
A little light with wings.

I never could have thought of it,
To have a little bug all lit
And made to go on wings.

—Elizabeth Madox Roberts

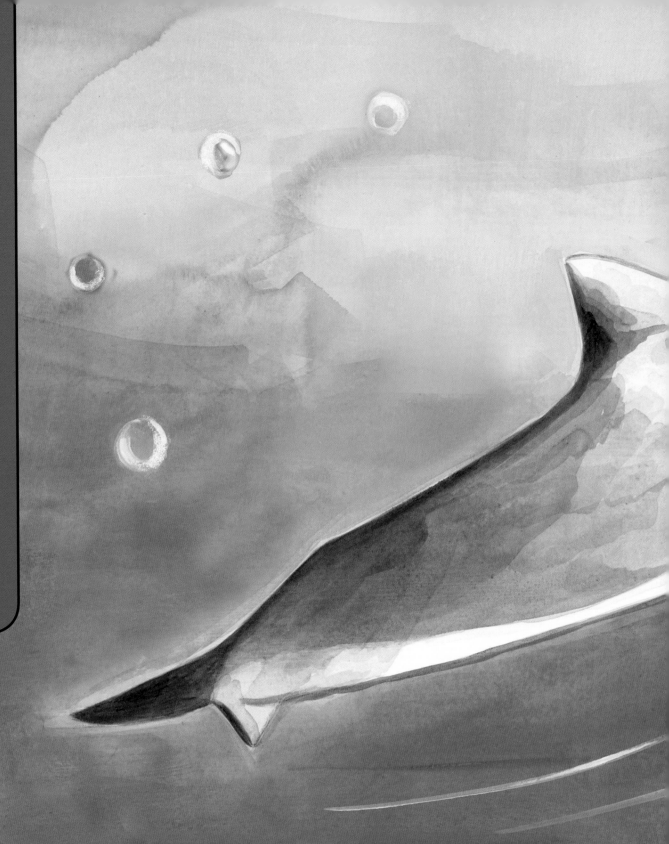

In rhyming poems, the rhythm is easy to see. But rhythm is important in poetry even if the words don't rhyme.

Look at the first two lines of "Sea Ribbons." The first line is long, with many hard and soft syllables. We spend some time reading it. We see the dolphin, and it seems to float in mid-air in front of us. The next line is very short. With three quick beats, we're plunging back into the water! The rhythm of each line matches what's happening in the poem.

Sea Ribbons

A dolphin soars into sparkling air and then
dives straight down
trailing a ribbon of silver bubbles that
echo her path, plunging,
spinning and funneling.

Racing up toward the sun, she
gathers speed for another joyous leap.

—Laura Purdie Salas

Piano

glossy black keys
clear white keys

step and rise
march in time

pairing up, sharing sounds
making music

—Laura Purdie Salas

As we saw earlier, rhyming poems often rhyme at the ends of lines. But rhyme can happen inside poems, too. And sometimes words don't rhyme exactly, but are alike enough to create a nice sound.

In "Piano," *rise* and *time* don't rhyme, but they come close. *Pairing* and *sharing* do rhyme, but they are inside the poem instead of at the ends of lines.

~ Tool 3 ~

In **ALLITERATION,** words start with the same letter sound.

Look at lines 3 to 6 of "Going to St. Ives." How many words start with an *s*? How many start with a *c* or *k*? Those are examples of alliteration.

Repeating letter sounds—no matter where they are in a word—makes a poem more fun to read. The words don't have to be right next to each other, but they should be nearby.

Going to St. Ives

1 As I was going to St. Ives

2 I met a man with seven wives.

3 Every wife had seven sacks,

4 Every sack had seven cats,

5 Every cat had seven kits.

6 Kits, cats, sacks, and wives,

7 How many were going to St. Ives?

~ Tool 4 ~

Sometimes, the best way to describe something is to compare it to something else. We can compare things using the words *like* or *as*. These comparisons are called **SIMILES**. For example, "It's as hot *as* an oven out there."

In the last four lines of "Fog," water is compared to curtains. This is a simile, because the word *like* is used.

Fog

Why is water as water
liquid diamonds
slices of brilliance

But water as fog
like pale theater curtains
opening inches before
your nose

—Laura Purdie Salas

~ Tool 5 ~

We can compare things without using any connecting words, too. We say something is something else. These comparisons are called **METAPHORS**. For example, "It's an oven out there."

In the first three lines of "Fog," water is compared to diamonds. This is a metaphor. Water isn't *like* liquid diamonds. It *is* liquid diamonds.

~ Tool 6 ~

Words that sound like what they mean are examples of **ONOMATOPOEIA.** These words can add interest and fun to a poem. *Swish, click, boom, hiccup, honk,* and *buzz* are all examples of onomatopoeia.

Beep!
Splash!
Cock-a-doodle-doo!

Free!

We are popcorn kernels
In class, waiting for the bell
Ready to explode
Full of heat, vibrating with energy

RRRIIIIIIIINNNNNNNNNNNNNG!

We
pop
Pop
POP

Out the doorway
Burst into the street
Fill the quiet with noise and motion

—Laura Purdie Salas

Free!

We are popcorn kernels
In class, waiting for the bell
Ready to explode
Full of heat, vibrating with energy

RRRIIIIIIINNNNNNNNNNNNNNNG!

We
POP
Pop
POP

Out the doorway
Burst into the street
Fill the quiet with noise and motion

—Laura Purdie Salas

"Free!" also gives us another example of using metaphor in poetry. Are kids in school really popcorn kernels? No—but they are alike in some ways. They both bounce with energy when they are set free. And in this case, the metaphor isn't limited to just a line or two. It's spread throughout the entire poem.

See how the extra space around the word *pop* makes it look like popcorn is flying across the page? The way words are laid out on the page is another way that poets add meaning to their work.

~ Tool 7 ~

The shape, or form, a poem takes is also a kind of tool poets use. An **ACROSTIC** is a bit like a puzzle. From top to bottom, the first letters of each line spell a word. But it's not just any word—it's the subject of the poem.

Here the first letters spell "spelling test," and the poem is about taking a spelling test.

The poem back on page 3 is an acrostic, too!

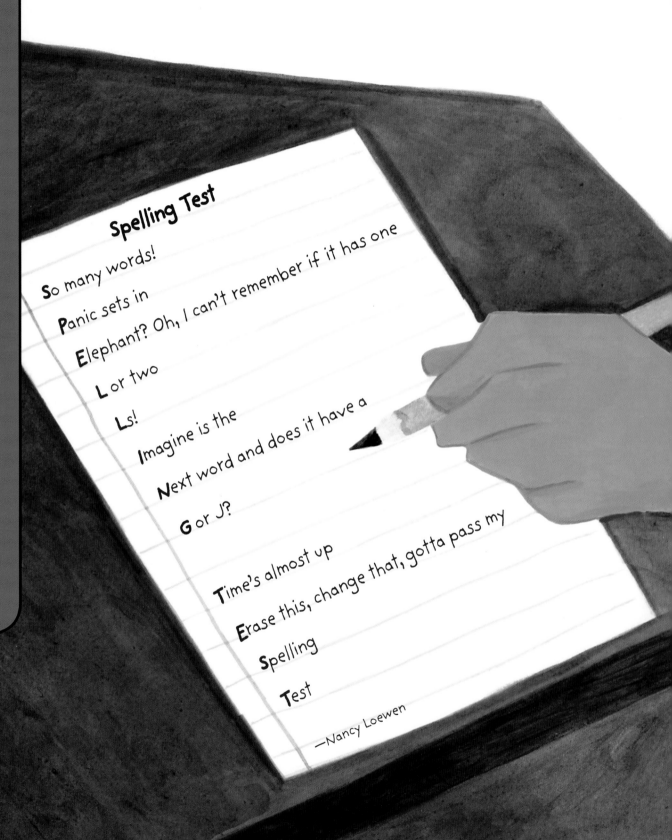

Spelling Test

So many words!

Panic sets in

Elephant? Oh, I can't remember if it has one

L or two

Ls!

Imagine is the

Next word and does it have a

G or J?

Time's almost up

Erase this, change that, gotta pass my

Spelling

Test

—Nancy Loewen

In Grandma's Barn

1 Kitten

2 Tiny nose, ears

3 Like snippets of soft felt

4 Eyes that will soon open for the

5 First time

—Nancy Loewen

~ Tool 9 ~

A **CONCRETE POEM** is a combination of poetry and art. These poems take the shape of their subjects. The actual words are still important—but so are what the words look like on the page.

The poem here is about a donut, and it looks like one, too!

The Capitol: More Than Just a Building

It's not the building that makes us strong
It's not the flag that promises freedom

Behind that flag
Inside that building

People like me
People like you

We make the Capitol
We make our country

—Laura Purdie Salas

~ Tool 10 ~

FREE VERSE POEMS don't rhyme. They don't have a set number of syllables or lines, either. The ideas in the poem help the poet decide how to write it.

We've already seen four free verse poems in this book: "Sea Ribbons" on page 11, "Piano" on page 12, "Fog" on page 17, and "Free!" on page 19.

~ Tool 11 ~

HAIKU is a very old kind of poetry from Japan. A haiku is usually about nature, especially the seasons. It shows us a picture, but it doesn't include many details. Readers are left feeling they have discovered something.

Haiku usually don't have titles. They are made up of three lines, with syllables arranged like this:

Line one: 5 syllables
Line two: 7 syllables
Line three: 5 syllables

1 Footprints in deep snow
2 Suddenly, the sweep of wings
3 An unknown angel

—Nancy Loewen

There was a Young Lady whose eyes,
Were unique as to color and size;
When she opened them wide,
People all turned aside,
And started away in surprise.

—Edward Lear

~ Tool 12 ~

A **LIMERICK** is a short, silly rhyming poem. It was named after the county of Limerick in Ireland.

Limericks have five lines. The first two lines rhyme with the last line. Here, for example, *eyes* and *size* rhyme with *surprise*. The third and fourth lines are shorter, and rhyme with each other—in this case, *wide* and *aside*.

The poem back on page 7 is a limerick, too!

Let's Review!

These are the **12 tools** you need to write great poetry.

In poetry, every word must be chosen carefully. Poets choose words not only for their meaning, but also for sound and RHYTHM **(1)**.

RHYME **(2)** often takes place at the ends of lines. But rhyming words might be used within lines, too. ALLITERATION **(3)** can add interest to a poem by repeating letter sounds.

Poems often compare one thing to another in an imaginative way. To do this, they may use SIMILES **(4)** or METAPHORS **(5)**.

ONOMATOPOEIA **(6)** can make a poem fun to read and fun to hear.

Some poetic forms have rules. They must rhyme a certain way or have a set number of syllables per line. Other forms don't have any rules at all. The poetic forms discussed in this book are: ACROSTIC **(7)**, CINQUAIN **(8)**, CONCRETE **(9)**, FREE VERSE **(10)**, HAIKU **(11)**, and LIMERICK **(12)**.

Getting Started Exercises

- Write an acrostic with your friends or classmates. Pick a word and write it on a piece of paper, going downward. Pass it around, letting every person add a line to the poem.

- Practice using similes and metaphors. Pick an object and describe it. Go into a lot of detail—but don't name the object. Now, give the list to a friend or two. Have them guess what you're describing. Did they think you were writing about something else? If so, do you see how different things can share some of the same qualities? Maybe you've got the start of a poem!

- Put together a poetry reading! Get your classmates together and listen to each other's work. If you want, you can pick a subject. Maybe all the poems should be about music, sports, or winter. Or you might want to pick a specific form, such as haiku or cinquain.

Writer's Tips

Keep a writing journal. As you go through your day, jot down the little things that you notice. Maybe the sky was pink this morning, or you saw a strange bird at the feeder. Maybe your baby sister said something that made you laugh. Your notes might someday become part of a poem.

Read your poetry out loud. (Record yourself, if possible.) Does it sound right? If you stumble over words, or the rhythm doesn't sound right, you might want to revise your work. (Revision is a big part of the writing process. Professional writers often revise their work many times.)

Find some poems you really like, and memorize them. The poems will be like good friends—always there when you need them.

If you're having trouble finishing a poem, put it away for a few days or weeks. When you come back to it, you might find that you know right away how to fix it.

Glossary

acrostic—a poem in which the first letters of each line spell out a word or phrase

alliteration—using several words that start with the same letter sound

cinquain—a five-line poem that follows a 2-4-6-8-2 pattern of syllables

compare—to look closely at things in order to discover ways they are alike or different

concrete poem—a poem that takes the shape of its subject

details—pieces of information; small parts of a bigger thing

free verse poem—a poem that follows no form or subject rules

haiku—a three-line poem that follows a 5-7-5 pattern of syllables

limerick—a silly five-line poem in which the first two lines rhyme with the last, and the third and fourth lines rhyme with each other

metaphor—a figure of speech that compares different things without using words such as *like* or *as*

onomatopoeia—words that copy the sound they are describing, such as *hiss*

revise, revision—to change something; to "re-vision" it, or see it in a new way

rhyme—word endings that sound the same

rhythm—a pattern of beats, like in music

simile—a figure of speech that compares different things using words such as *like* or *as*

syllable—a small unit of language that includes a vowel sound; a syllable is like a beat in music

To Learn More

More Books to Read

Fletcher, Ralph. *Poetry Matters: Writing a Poem from the Inside Out.* New York: HarperTrophy, 2002.

Fletcher, Ralph. *A Writing Kind of Day: Poems for Young Poets.* Honesdale, Pa.: Wordsong/Boyds Mills Press, 2005.

Prelutsky, Jack. *Pizza, Pigs, and Poetry: How to Write a Poem.* New York: Greenwillow Books, 2008.

On the Web

FactHound offers a safe, fun way to find educator-approved Internet sites related to this book.

Here's what you do:

1. Visit *www.facthound.com*
2. Choose your grade level.
3. Begin your search.

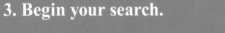

This book's ID number is 9781404853447

Index

Look for all of the books in the Writer's Toolbox series:

Once Upon a Time: Writing Your Own Fairy Tale
Show Me a Story: Writing Your Own Picture Book
Sincerely Yours: Writing Your Own Letter
Words, Wit, and Wonder: Writing Your Own Poem